Cambridge Early Years

Let's Explore

Learner's Book 3B

Kathryn Harper

Contents

Note to parents and practitioners					3

## Block 3: Caring for ourselves and the world		4

## Block 4: Then and now							18

Acknowledgements								32

Note to parents and practitioners

This Learner's Book provides activities to support the second term of Let's Explore for Cambridge Early Years 3.

Activities can be used at school or at home. Children will need support from an adult. Additional guidance about activities can be found in the **For practitioners** boxes.

Some activities use stickers. The stickers can be found in the middle of this book.

Stories are provided for children to enjoy looking at and listening to. Children are not expected to be able to read the stories themselves.

Children will encounter the following characters within this book. You could ask children to point to the characters when they see them on the pages, and say their names.

The Learner's Book activities support the Teaching Resource activities. The Teaching Resource provides step-by-step coverage of the Cambridge Early Years curriculum and guidance on how the Learner's Book activities develop the curriculum learning statements.

Hi, my name is Mia.

Find us on the front covers doing lots of fun activities.

Hi, my name is Gemi.

Hi, my name is Rafi.

Hi, my name is Kiho.

Block 3
Caring for ourselves and the world

Our community
Choose stickers and say.

For practitioners
Children explore the picture and discuss what they can see. Children put the stickers in the correct place, e.g., the fruit stand in front of the greengrocer. Point to Mia and read the question aloud. Discuss children's answers. Encourage children to find Mia in the picture.

Snack time!
Draw and say.

For practitioners
Children identify the foods in the picture. Talk about making healthy food choices. Children draw balanced meals on the characters' plates, choosing from the food options in the pantry. Talk about how eating a balanced diet is important for a healthy body.

How do you keep healthy?
Colour.

● ○ ○ not often   ● ● ○ sometimes   ● ● ● always

I eat fruits and vegetables.
○ ○ ○

I drink lots of water.
○ ○ ○

I warm up before exercise.
○ ○ ○

I run and jump!
○ ○ ○

I get lots of sleep.
○ ○ ○

For practitioners
Children colour in circles to show how often they do each healthy habit. You may need to explain the meaning of *often*, *sometimes* and *always*. Discuss children's answers, and help them to understand what they need to do if their answer is ever 'not often'.

Choose a kitchen

Spot the difference.

Look at the pictures. Find the five differences.

For practitioners

Children circle the five differences in the pictures. Ask *Which kitchen is more environmentally friendly? Why?* You could also talk about safety and tidiness.

How can we look after our world?

Write and say.

Match the problems with the correct solutions.

Problems

 Our cars use lots of petrol.

 We use lots of electricity.

 We waste water.

 Plastic is harming the oceans and the creatures that live in it.

Solutions

 1 Recycle plastic.

 2 Walk to places where possible.

 3 Turn off lights when we are not using them.

 4 Turn off water when we have finished using it.

For practitioners

In pairs, children look at the first set of images and discuss why these are problems. Provide support if necessary. Then children look at the solutions and decide which one works best to resolve each problem. They can also suggest more solutions.

Water quiz
Read and circle.

1		Ice is frozen water.	Yes	No
2		Polar bears live in ponds.	Yes	No
3		Animals do not drink water.	Yes	No
4		Plants need water.	Yes	No
5		We wash our clothes with sand.	Yes	No
6		Water comes from the sun.	Yes	No

For practitioners
Read the sentences aloud and ensure children understand them. Children work individually or in pairs to decide if the sentences are right or wrong, making suggestions to correct the sentences if they are wrong.

Where is the Water?
Read and draw.

1 "What's wrong Bear?" asks Fox.

"There's no water for a bath. Now I'm very itchy," says Bear.

2 "There's no clean water to drink," says Fox. "Now I'm unwell from the dirty water."

3 Deer is feeling weak. "The river has no water," she says. "No grass grows. I am hungry."

"Where is the clean water?" asks Bear. "Let's ask Beaver."

4

"Where is the water?" ask Bear, Fox and Deer.

"Oh," says Beaver. "Follow me."

5 The animals follow the beaver up the hill, down the hill, through the field …

6 Then they arrive at a beautiful pond.

"Clean water!" cry Bear and Fox.

"This pond is new," says Deer.

7 "Yes," says Beaver. "Look at my dam! It stops the water."

"But it's stopping the water flowing into the river," says Deer.

"Sorry," says Beaver. "Let me see …"

8 Beaver pulls out some branches.

"Look! The water is flowing again," says Beaver.

"Now we can all have clean water," says Deer.

"Let's swim!" cries Bear.

For practitioners

Read *Where is the Water?* Ask children about what the animals in the story needed. What else needed water in the story (grass)? Children then choose a character. Ask *What does bear/fox/beaver/deer do next?* Children can use their drawing to perform a role-play in small groups.

Water and land

Look and colour.

For practitioners

Explain that this is a map of Earth, the planet we live on. Ask *Which part is the water? Which part is the land?* Children colour in the water and land features. Ask children whether they think there is more water or land on Earth. Ask *Do you know what the land is made of?* Explain that there is water than land on Earth and the land is made of rock and soil. Encourage children to say what they know about the animals and where they live.

Label the map
Write.

road   river   station   school   bridge   park   beach   hospital

For practitioners
Look at the map. Discuss the different outdoor environments and features. Children look at the word pool, identify each feature on the map and write a label in the space provided. You may need to offer support by reading the words aloud for the children.

Stickers for pages 4–5

Stickers for pages 18-19

What can you remember?
Read and write.

1

2

☐ This is mostly covered by water.

☐ We should remember to turn this off.

☐ We need to recycle this.

☐ We need to drink lots of this.

☐ These are good for us.

3

4

5

For practitioners
Read the statements aloud for the children.. Children write numbers to match the statements to the correct picture. Discuss each of the statements. Ask *Why is it important for us to take care of ourselves and our world?*

Block 4 Then and now

Old and new
Choose stickers and say.

For practitioners
Children explore the picture and put the stickers in the correct places, e.g., the family photo on the wall. Point to Kiho and read the question aloud. Ask *Where is Kiho?* Encourage children to find Kiho in the picture. Ask children what they know about what their parents did when they were children. Did they play with the same toys/play the same games/listen to the same music?

What do you know about your family?

Write.

1 Choose your family member.
  There are some examples below.

My mother   My dad   My grandmother   My carer

2 Where did they grow up?

_____

3 What games did they play?

_____

4 What was their favourite food?

_____

For practitioners

Children choose a family member or significant carer. Children write answers to the questions and then draw a picture of their family member or carer as a child. Children could complete this at home, asking their family member the questions.

My timeline

Match and say.

I am a baby.

I am an adult.

I go to school.

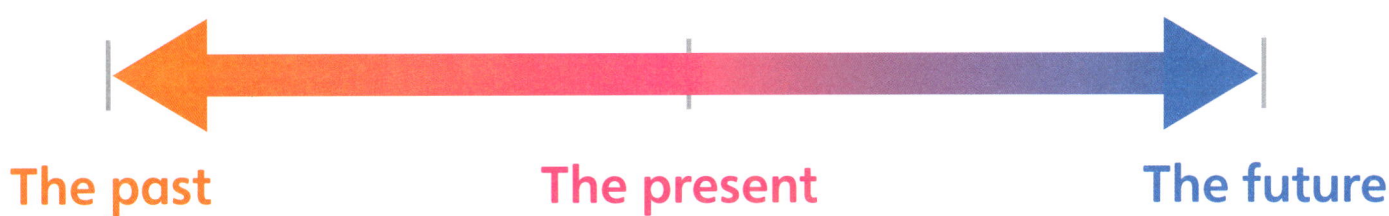

The past　　　　　**The present**　　　　　**The future**

When I grow up, I want to be _____ .

For practitioners

Ensure that children understand how the timeline works. Explain that it is about their own experiences. Talk about the labels. Children draw lines to match the labels to different points on the timeline: the past, present, or future. Then they say or write what they want to be when they grow up.

What's new?
Find and stick.

Then	Now
 an aeroplane  a car  a bicycle  a lorry  a bus	

For practitioners
Talk about the old forms of transport in the pictures, then ask children about the ones we see today. If possible, children use the internet to find pictures of these from the present, print them out and stick them into the table. Alternatively, they could draw pictures using internet images as inspiration. Ask children to compare the images. Ask *What are the similarities and differences?*

Funny car
Draw.

For practitioners
Talk about cars from the past and the present. Children then draw a car using their imagination that can have features of old and new cars, or be something entirely new. Encourage children to compare their finished drawings and to vote for the most creative car.

How does sound travel?
Match.

 That is too quiet.

 That is too loud!

For practitioners
Read each speech bubble and ask *Who is closest to the music? Why do you think that?* Explain that the closer you are to a sound, the louder it is. Children match the person to the source of the sound by following the lines of the maze.

Snakes and ladders
Play.

For practitioners
Children play in pairs or small groups. You will need to provide a die, and coins or small toys to use as counters. Children take it in turns to roll the die, moving their counter as many squares as spots on the die. If they land on a ladder, they climb it, moving up the grid. If they land on a snake, they move back down. The first child to reach the END square wins.

What is their favourite song?

Listen and write.

1 What is your favourite song?

   _____

2 Is your favourite song soft, medium or fast? Circle.

   slow   medium   fast

3 Do you like soft, medium or loud music? Circle.

   soft   medium   **LOUD**

4 Is the song high, medium or low? Circle.

   high   medium   low

5 How does the song make you feel? Circle or write a word.

   happy   sad   relaxed   excited   thoughtful

   _____

> **For practitioners**
> Children can complete this activity at home, asking a family member the questions. If possible, the family member should play the piece of music, ideally from the past, for the child to hear. Remind children of what terms such as *dynamics* (loudness), *tempo* (speed), *pitch*, *rhythm* and *pulse* mean.

The Hokey Cokey

Draw.

You put your  in, your  out,

In, out, in, out, shake it all about.

You do the Hokey Cokey and you turn around.

That's what it's all about!

Chorus:

Oh, oh, the Hokey Cokey!

Oh, oh, the Hokey Cokey!

Oh, oh, the Hokey Cokey!

Knees bent, arms stretched, ra, ra, ra!

You put your  in, your  out,

In, out, in, out, shake it all about.

You do the Hokey Cokey and you turn around.

That's what it's all about!

(Chorus)

You put your  in, your  out,

In, out, in, out, you shake it all about.

You do the Hokey Cokey and you turn around.

That's what it's all about!

All together now!

(Chorus)

You put your in, your out,

In (woo), out (woo), shake it all about.

You do the Hokey Cokey and you turn around.

That's what it's all about!

Wait for it (woo ...)

(Chorus)

And that's that!

For practitioners

Children draw pictures to complete the verses. They must think of new words to go with the song, drawing the body parts that the movements relate to. Tell them that they can specify *right* and *left*. Then children teach their version to a partner or family member.

Maze navigation

Draw lines and say.

For practitioners
Children complete the maze by reuniting the single skittle with the group of skittles, and the single marble with the group of marbles. Explain that children can ask you for help if they need it. Encourage them to use a pencil first. Ask children who have completed the maze to share how they did it to help others. Ask children if they know any other games that people played in the past.

Review game

Play.

You can use:

Roll and move this number of spaces.

GO!		You find an old photo of your grandmother. Go forward 2 spaces. 
You make a poster of old and new boats. Go forward 2 spaces. 		You stepped on your train model. Go back 1 space. 
PAUSE		You show your grandmother a new streaming service. Go forward 2 spaces.
Your mum teaches you a traditional dance. Go forward 1 space. 		You share some memories with your grandfather. Go forward 2 spaces. 
PAUSE		You learn to skip. Go forward 1 space. 

For practitioners

Children play in pairs. They each move their counter forwards or backwards, depending on the instructions in each square. If children land on a blank square, they must stay there and miss a turn. This game reviews the different things children learnt about during this block and provides a prompt for reflection and sharing experiences.

You found your mum's old guitar. Go forward 3 spaces. 	You lost your first teddy bear. Go back 1 space. 	PAUSE
You learn to use an old phone. Go forward 1 space. 	The old television doesn't work. Go back 2 spaces. 	You went on an old train. Go forward 1 space. 
You lose the computer game to your mum. Go back 3 spaces.  	You make an amazing picture on your computer. Go forward 1 space.	You listen to some beautiful music. Go forward 2 spaces. 
PAUSE	You create a fantastic dance! Go forward 3 spaces. 	You fall down during *The Hokey Cokey*. Go back 2 spaces. 
You don't pin the tail on the donkey. Go back 3 spaces.  	Your dad sings his favourite song. Go back 1 space. 	You win! 

Acknowledgements

The authors and publishers acknowledge the following sources of copyright material and are grateful for the permissions granted. While every effort has been made, it has not always been possible to identify the sources of all the material used, or to trace all copyright holders. If any omissions are brought to our notice, we will be happy to include the appropriate acknowledgements on reprinting.

Thanks to the following for permission to reproduce images: p9 George Pachantouris/GI, Catherine Falls Commercial/GI, LisaValder/GI, ArtMarie/GI, Yasser Chalid/GI, lomography/GI, Steven Puetzer/GI, Alexander Ipfelkofer/GI; p10 Peter Dazeley/GI, Belfalah Soufian/500px/GI, Vicki Jauron, Babylon and Beyond Photography/GI, Blue Planet Studio/GI, Radnatt/GI, Peter Cade/GI; p17 Stocktrek Images/GI, gaffera/GI, MARINA BOGACHYOVA/GI, I Like That One/GI, DonoMacs/GI; p23 Anton_Sokolov/GI, NNehring/GI, frankix/GI, Marcia Straub/GI, ewg3D/GI

Key: GI = Getty Images

Thanks to the following artists at Beehive Illustration:
Veronika Chaves, Katharine Henry, Tamara Joubert, Carl Pearce, Sarah Pitt, Elisa Rochi.

Cover characters by Becky Davies (The Bright Agency)